Cactus Jack Gaxter = ?
?–1894

Humperdinck Grandmother
Bummer = Bummer
1866–1920   1867–1918

O'Boile

Eff   = Ortrud Patrick Sean Earwig
?75– | 1882– 1888– 1891– 1894–
961 | 1942   1932   1952   1956

Otho   = Molassa   Abner
1876–1941 | 1878–1929   1888–1966

Hamilton   Antigone
1901–1946   1904–1937

J. Bummer Gaxter = Little Dipper
1899–1951   ?–?

Murk
16–1958

Jasper
1920–1969

Remarkable Relatives

Cousin J. Bummer Gaxter

Remarkable Relatives

by John Train

 Clarkson N. Potter, Inc./Publishers
Distributed by Crown Publishers, Inc. New York

Inquiries should be addressed to Clarkson N. Potter, Inc., One Park Avenue, New York, New York 10016

Printed in the United States of America

Published simultaneously in Canada by General Publishing Company Limited

Library of Congress Cataloging in Publication Data

Train, John.
  Remarkable relatives.

  1. Genealogy—Anecdotes, facetiae, satire, etc.
I. Title.
PN6231.G38T7   1981   818'.5402   81-8673
ISBN: 0-517-54542X   AACR2

10 9 8 7 6 5 4 3 2 1

First Edition

Preface

The history of our family and of our investment firm are intertwined. For almost a century we have served our clientele through many changes — mostly bad — in our town of Hooton, Mass., and in the world: from the Scylla of socialism to the Charybdis of . . . whatever.

From time to time family members, friends, customers, and employees have asked about our origins. Frankly, I knew little beyond occasional references in the standard texts.* Fortunately, Mrs. Cedric Mebbs, my great-aunt, devoted her years of widowhood to the subject. I take pleasure in updating her work and offering it to a wider audience.

J.T.

*See *Cancers of Wall Street,* Scribner's, 1910, pp. 81–82, 101ff., 174, 216.

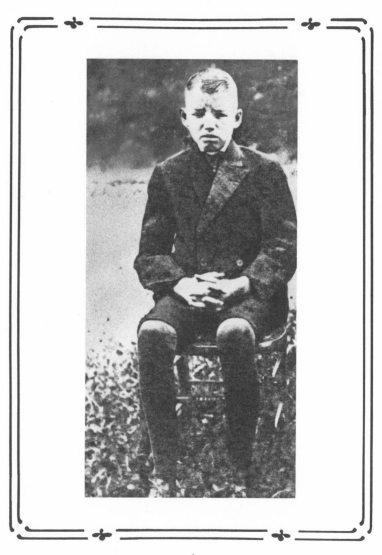

The author as a lad, wearing horsehair trousers, during the Grecian Pageant interlude in sister Pagoda's graduation ceremony from the Hooton Female Academy.

I attended a modest boarding school in Groton, Mass., presided over by Dr. Teargash. He believed in corporal punishment for any misbehavior, as I found out when he caught me doing an imitation of him picking his nose. Every boy is a bad boy, he maintained. Many ran away, reinforcing his conviction.

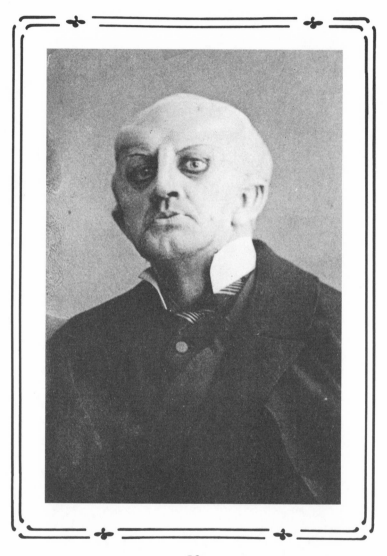

Professor Wartkopf, who claimed to have
fought on both sides in the Russian
Revolution, taught me French and
Esperanto.
Here he demonstrates the French "u,"
which he claimed no other faculty member
could pronounce correctly.

*My grandfather, the Judge, Pontius P.
Train.*

*He sometimes kept the lawyers waiting
while he indulged his passion for marine
mammals, notably dolphins and walruses,
at the Hooton Aquarium. Entering the
pool, he would frolic with his finny friends
by the hour.*

*Eventually he waxed his mustaches
forward like walrus tusks.*

*In his last years a surprise visit would
usually find him disporting himself in his
private tank.*

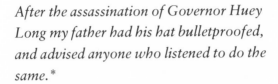

After the assassination of Governor Huey Long my father had his hat bulletproofed, and advised anyone who listened to do the same. *

---

* When Queen Marie visited Boston in 1902, among the notables assembled to greet her on the platform stood Gramps and my father, then a small boy. The train arrived and gasped to a stop. Two hours dragged by. Still the queen failed to emerge.

After whispered consultations several strong men stuffed my father through a window of the queen's compartment. Moments later, sweating slightly but with a radiant smile, she descended, leading him by the hand. In sight of all, she handed him a cash reward.

It seemed that she had trapped herself in the toilet. My father, injected into the tiny chamber, had forced the door with a savage kick, saving the day.

The reward, reinvested, eventually constituted most of our firm's capital.

Pontius Train's sister, Teeny, married
Cedric Mebbs, a clergyman of Rutland,
Vermont.
Cedric's high, reedy voice and chronic
laryngitis rendered him inaudible from the
pulpit, especially in winter, when his flock
suffered from respiratory complaints of
their own.
The congregation dwindled . . . to a dozen,
then two couples, and at last to empty
pews.
After three seasons of sermons preached to
the four walls, he renounced the cloth.

Cousin Teeny was famous for her herbal remedies. She made Cedric drink a gallon of nettle juice daily for his vocal cords. As a result he grew paler and paler, and his voice increasingly squeaky. *

---

* She edited Cedric's sermons for publication (C. Mebbs, *Celestial Intimations*, vols. I– XXIII, privately printed), and assembled most of these photographs, which she then left to me; her house and half an acre on the edge of Rutland she bequeathed to her faithful housekeeper, Aunt Jelloe.

"Aunt" Jelloe, the Mebbs's faithful housekeeper, was convinced that one should insert corks into faucets after turning them off. Applying a scissor to the sockets, she occasionally tried to trim the wicks of electric lamps, with spectacular consequences.

After Teeny died, Jelloe spent her days on the porch, rocking. As Rutland expanded, Jelloe found herself rocking away in the heart of the business district. Realtors approached her with attractive propositions, but Jelloe, mistaking their purpose, shooed them off.

Romeo Mebbs, like his father interested in public speaking, pursued home study courses in elocution, practicing for hours before the mirror.

*His rendition of Burke's attack in Parliament on Warren Hastings (at the end of which Burke falls fainting into the arms of his friend Sheridan) brought tears to all eyes.** *

* He sometimes directed this number against the family hound, Digger, dreaming peacefully of summer and bones in his accustomed place by the fire. Digger would awake, see everyone staring at him while Uncle Romeo shook his fists and thundered, and slink out hurriedly.

*Terrible-tempered Uncle Julius, the other
son of Cedric and Teeny Mebbs, became a
fervent vivisectionist.**

* He illustrated the adage about clergymen's chil-
dren. When he married, his bride's younger sister
accompanied the happy pair on their honeymoon
trip around the Gaspé Peninsula. There was con-
sternation when both ladies became pregnant, but
the outbreak of World War I usurped public at-
tention.

At his wife's burial his stage whisper — "It's time
for lunch! I wish he'd hurry up!" — so rattled the
minister that he omitted part of the ceremony.

Young Ollie Mebbs never came back from his trip around the world.

In response to advertisements placed by the family in the Straits Times *and the* South China Mail, *offers* were received from various quarters for his return, but in all cases Uncle Julius felt that the ransom proposed was excessive.*

---

* One fragment, which I have before me now, torn and discolored and accompanied by a desiccated ear, reads: "Dumb boy . . . twelve gold pieces . . . finger . . ."

Cousin Luscious Mebbs as a member of Delta Delta Upsilon — shortly before he lost his mind.

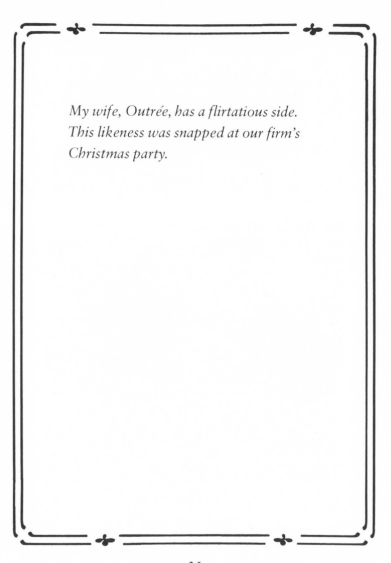

My wife, Outrée, has a flirtatious side.
This likeness was snapped at our firm's
Christmas party.

Outrée's father, Théophobe Arsénique
Pompard, settled in Hooton after a
misunderstanding with the authorities in
Marseilles, France.
He offered instruction in French language
and customs, including, it was rumored,
certain intimate cultural practices.

Like Outrée herself, her brother Murk
(here shown on their trip to the pyramids),
while painstakingly turned out,
occasionally misses the spirit of the
occasion.

Blanco Swingle, who left Divinity School to become an actor, was my rival for Outrée's favors.*

His distinguished profile brought him renown on the stage, until it was discovered that he had an uncontrollable tic on the left side of his face.

---

* His hobby was taxidermy, and as tributes he used to bring her his creations: a pair of stuffed owls, a cleverly mounted lizard, and the like. They had to be carried down from the attic whenever he came to call, which did not help his cause.

*Mother was regularly voted one of
Hooton's best-dressed women, to my
father's satisfaction.
She would say of a rival, "But her shoes are
atrocious," thus reminding one discreetly
of her vast collection.*

My mother's father, Commander Hannibal Gridlock.
Neither enemy fire nor the perils of the deep ended his career, but strangulation, when an overzealous orderly finally succeeded in fastening his choke collar.*

* The commander was with Commodore Dewey
  in Manila Bay when the commodore started the
  Spanish-American War with the celebrated words,
  "You may fire when you are ready, Gridlock."
     Many historians have the commodore saying,
  "You may fire when you are ready, Gridley."
  Probably, distracted by the smoke and din of battle,
  they garbled their account. After all, assuming
  Hannibal's finger was on the trigger, what one
  really heard would have been, "You may fire when
  you are ready, Grid . . . *BOOM!*"

Cactus Jack Gaxter, the patriarch of my mother's side of the family, was scalped by the Shoshoni. Although he bought a toupee, when in polite company he was embarrassed to take off his hat. As a result, he rarely came indoors — in fact, almost never.

Cactus Jack's eldest son, Uncle Eff Gaxter,
had a successful career as a high-pressure
salesman.
Retiring to Delaware Water Gap, he
revealed important plans for the town: a
Changing of the Guard ceremony at the
Water Works to lure tourists; a factory to
make amphibious horse-drawn vehicles.
He hired my brother-in-law, Murk, to help
him work out the details, and got my father
and Uncle Otho to put up some money.
Thus our family firm got off to a flying
start.

Eff's wife, Ortrud, née O'Boile, saw little need for diversions of any kind. Indeed, she claimed not to know where her own daughter, Antigone, had come from.

An early suffragette, Antigone carried the doctrine of women's liberation to the Flan Indians of the upper Amazon. Eventually, sick of her hectoring, the matrons of the village ate her.

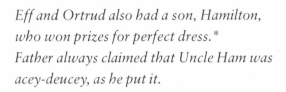

*Eff and Ortrud also had a son, Hamilton,
who won prizes for perfect dress.*
Father always claimed that Uncle Ham was
acey-deucey, as he put it.*

* He was devoted to his clubs: the Saturday Thes-
pians, the Musketeers, the Dinkelhouser Street
Irregulars, the Squirrel, the Fife and Fum, the
Boosters.

His obituary in the *Daily Gap* started: "DEATH OF
CLUBMAN. Mr. Hamilton Gaxter died last night at
his home here. His clubs included the American
Automobile Association . . ."

Ortrud had three brothers, Patrick, Sean, and Earwig. Patrick grew faster than the others. Indeed, he developed an impressive physique.*

* As it happened, Patrick couldn't hold down any job for more than a few weeks, while Sean and Earwig, although of less than average height, both prospered. Sean, not long after this photograph was taken, attained celebrity as the "Boy Mayor of Minneapolis."

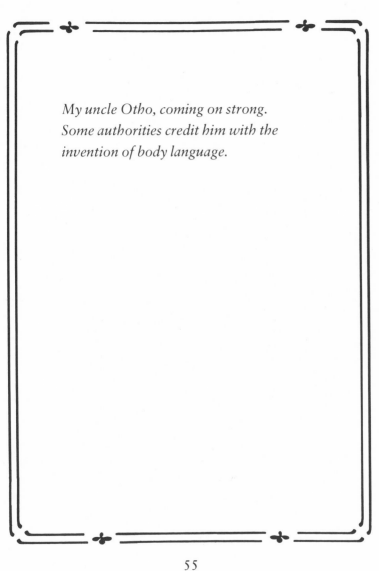

My uncle Otho, coming on strong.
Some authorities credit him with the
invention of body language.

Otho's wife, Molassa, eventually renounced her teaching position to give full time to her hair.

Molassa as an infant

Molassa's father, Humperdinck Bummer, who lived in the nearby town of Flynn, Mass., had a respectable career in public life. His wife resembled him closely enough to take his place on the pumper if illness prevented him from performing his official functions.

Jasper Gaxter, the voyeur, was generally
thought to be the natural offspring of
Monsieur Pompard. Once Aunt Ortrud
caught him peering in her window, which
she smashed down on his fingers so sharply
that he wore a cast for months.
Later he started a successful model agency.

Cousin Abner Bummer was Otho's brother-in-law. When the first streetcar came to Hooton, he applied for the position of conductor (rear). Although the passengers were helpful, he remained confused by all the different coins.
He was Aunt Jelloe's favorite in the family. She considered him "folks."
When she left him her property, by then worth almost a million dollars, he accepted Uncle Eff as his financial adviser. Later, my father took over the job, and I succeeded him. Abner became a silent partner of our firm — the only one to appear regularly at meetings in uniform.

Index

Amazon (upper), 49
"Aunt" Jelloe, 19n, 20, 21, 63

Boston, 15n
Bummer, Abner, 62, 63
Bummer, Grandmother, 59
Bummer, Humperdinck, 58, 59
Burke, Edmund, 23

Cancers of Wall Street, 5n
Celestial Intimations, 19n

Daily Gap, 51n
Delaware Water Gap, 45
Delta Delta Epsilon, 29
Dewey, Commodore George, 41n
Digger, 23n

Esperanto, 11

Family investment firm, 5, 31, 45, 63
Flan Indians, 49
Flynn, Mass., 59

Gaspé Peninsula, 25n
Gaxter, Antigone, 47, 48, 49
Gaxter, Cactus Jack, 42, 43, 45
Gaxter, Eff, 44, 45, 51, 63
Gaxter, Hamilton, 50, 51
Gaxter, J. Bummer, 2
Gaxter, Jasper, 60, 61
Gaxter, Molassa (Mrs. Otho), 56, 57, 59
Gaxter, Ortrud (Mrs. Eff), 46, 47, 51, 53, 61
Gaxter, Otho, 45, 54, 55, 57
Gridlock, Commander Hannibal, 40, 41
Groton, Mass., 9

Hastings, Warren, 23
Hooton, Mass., 5, 33, 39, 63
Hooton Aquarium, 13
Hooton Female Academy, 7

Long, Governor Huey, 15

Manila Bay, 41n
Marie, Queen, 15n
Marseilles, France, 33
Mebbs, Cedric, 16, 17, 19, 23, 25
Mebbs, Luscious, 28, 29
Mebbs, Ollie, 26, 27
Mebbs, Romeo, 22, 23
Mebbs, Teeny (Mrs. Cedric), 5, 17, 18, 19, 21, 25
Mebbs, Terrible-tempered Julius, 24, 25, 27
Minneapolis, Minn., 53n
Mother, 38, 39, 41

O'Boile, Earwig, 52, 53
O'Boile, Patrick, 52, 53
O'Boile, Sean, 52, 53

Pompard, Murk, 34, 35, 45
Pompard, Théophobe Arsénique, 32, 33, 61
Pyramids, 35

Russian Revolution, 11
Rutland, Vermont, 17, 19n, 21

Sheridan, Richard Brinsley, 23
Shoshoni Indians, 43
South China Mail, 27
Spanish-American War, 41n
Straits Times, 27
Swingle, Blanco, 36, 37

Teargash, Dr., 8, 9
Train, Hippophagus, 14, 15, 45, 51, 63
Train, John, 5, 6, 7, 9, 63
Train, Judge Pontius P., 12, 13
Train, Outrée (Mrs. John), 30, 31, 35, 37
Train, Pagoda, 7

Wartkopf, Professor, 10, 11
World War I, 25n